Wolfgang Amadeus

MOZART

Andante

from **Piano Concerto No. 21**
in C major, KV467

as used in the motion picture

Elvira Madigan

Sergei

RACHMANINOV

Highlights from

Piano Concerto No. 2
in C minor, op. 18

as used in the motion picture

Brief Encounter

3093

Suggestions for using this MMO edition

We have tried to create a product that will provide you an easy way to learn and perform a concerto with a full orchestra in the comfort of your own home. The following MMO features and techniques will help you maximize the effectiveness of the MMO practice and performance system:

Where the soloist begins a movement *solo*, we have provided an introductory measure with subtle taps inserted at the actual tempo before the soloist's entrance.

Chapter stops on your CD are conveniently located throughout the piece at the beginnings of practice sections, and are cross-referenced in the score. This should help you quickly find a desired place in the music as you learn the piece.

We have observed generally accepted tempi, but some may wish to perform at a different tempo, or to slow down or speed up the accompaniment for practice purposes. In addition to the slow-tempo selections included in this package, you can purchase from MMO specialized CD players which allow variable speed while maintaining proper pitch. This is an indispensable tool for the serious musician and you may wish to look into purchasing this useful piece of equipment for full enjoyment of all your MMO editions.

We want to provide you with the most useful practice and performance accompaniments possible. If you have any suggestions for improving the MMO system, please feel free to contact us. You can reach us by e-mail at *info@musicminusone.com*.

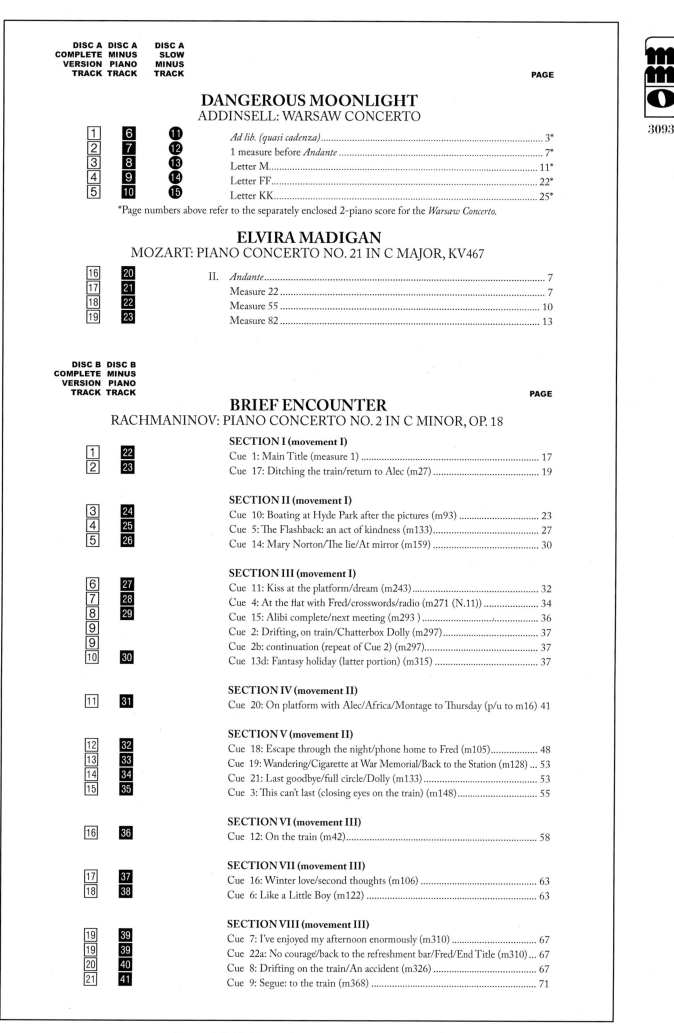

ISBN 1-59615-818-2
978-1-59615-818-4

MMO 3093

3093

Mozart's Piano Concerto in C major, kv467 'Elvira Madigan'

Unquestionably one of the most romantic movements in any piano concerto composed by Mozart—or by any other composer, for that matter—is the second movement of his Piano Concerto No. 21 in C Major, KV467, the dreamlike *Andante*. Here, Mozart masterfully merges marked dissonances and muted strings with a fluid melody, sung aria-like over continuous triplets and pizzicato strings, creating a deceptively simple, magical sound which hangs suspended in the heavens.

This *Andante* has for many years been identified with the 1967 Swedish film *Elvira Madigan,* which drew its theme from this movement. The film's story revolves around the life of the actual nineteenth-century Danish circus performer Elvira Madigan (1867-1889), and her ultimately fatal affair with a Swedish officer, Sixten Sparre. Though the film itself is not commonly known today, the reintroduction to its audiences' ears of Mozart's C-major concerto has left a lasting impression, and its title seems to have become bonded to the work, and vice versa.

In this *Andante*, Mozart is exposed on the brink of the forthcoming period in art, Romanticism, in which personal expression becomes paramount, and in which Classicism's emphasis on symmetry and balance became superceded by a much looser form. In this *Andante's* extraordinary slowness, Mozart single-handedly appears to be breaking with music's past and present, and to be looking forward to an entirely new sensibility. Despite its slow reflectiveness, there is an atmosphere of radiant sunlight, charmingly dappled, which shines forth beautifully.

※ ※

A measure of confusion hovers over the composition dates for the concerto. While Mozart has been criticized for not keeping a cleaner and more accurate catalogue of his works, one is tempted to say, rather, that it is all the more remarkable he came as close as he did in keeping his catalogue even remotely systematized. After all, his output was overwhelming and his composition-speed phenomenal. And, besides—what if Mozart had indeed kept a better, thoroughly accurate catalogue? How then would the legion of Mozartian scholars these past two centuries have spent their time and earned their income?

The autograph manuscript of KV467, which resides in the Morgan Library in New York, is dated "nel Febraio 1785" ("in February 1785"), while in his catalogue Mozart had entered 9 March 1785. This confusion can be easily settled if we assume the February 1785 date refers to the month Mozart began the composition while 9 March was the exact date of completion. Since this latter date happened to be the day before the work's initial performance, on 10 March 1785, we can also assume Mozart worked under the gun composing the concerto up to the very last moment.

Which is all to say that Mozart must have composed this masterpiece of the piano concerto form in a short span of about twenty-seven days. This came right after the completion of his previous masterwork, the Piano Concerto No. 20 in D minor, KV466, on 10 February. The almost total lack of revisions in the autograph score of KV467 illustrates for us what books and lectures about Mozart can only hollowly scratch at—that this composer's brilliance was of the most profound order. To realize that this magnificent concerto could have poured forth from any human with such little apparent effort is to understand the meaning of true genius.

We must not for a moment assume that this busiest of composers had sequestered himself during the four weeks of the work's composition. Far from it. Mozart taught pupils on a daily basis during this period; endured a long, draining visit from his unusually demanding father, Leopold; held a quartet-party to play through with his father and with Franz Josef Haydn some of Mozart's new quartets dedicated to that Classical master; participated in at least a dozen private and public concerts; and had to play his usual rôle of husband and breadwinner. With this schedule it is no wonder Mozart found so little time for revising his works. What is more remarkable is that he found the time to compose anything at all.

But compose Mozart did, as was demanded by the desperate need to pay his eternally mounting debts. Leopold reported that his son took in 559 gulden for the concerto, a sum that must have seemed good enough to the composer at the time, though it reeks of absurdity now.

A handbill announcing the première of KV467 on 10 March 1785 states that Mozart was to play the work himself. The handbill also states that the concerto was to be played on an "especially large Forte piano pedale." This interesting instrument had been custom-built by Mozart for his Viennese concerts, and he used it to reinforce the lower notes in his piano concerti and in improvising fantasias. It was essentially a legless fortepiano that lay on the floor underneath his usual piano. He played it with the feet by means of a pedal-board, very much like an organ is played. Since Mozart was a skilled organist, playing such a bizarre configuration must have come easily to him. Though we may not quite be able to experience the net effect of that particular performance, the piece remains one of the composer's most memorable.

—*Douglas Scharmann*

Excerpt from the Preface to the 1886 Bischoff Edition†

THE PRINCIPAL SOURCE for this edition of the C-major Concerto was the autograph of the score, belonging to Conductor-in-Chief W. Taubert. Besides the above, I collated the old Breitkopf & Härtel edition of the parts, an early André engraved edition of the piano-part, Richault's score-edition, the score-edition published by André* in 1855, the new Breitkopf & Härtel edition of the score (Series XVI, 21), and other modern editions.

The autograph is dated "Febraio 1785." Although it contains many passages which are "written over," the text is, with few exceptions, nowhere doubtful. Some disputed points are discussed in the Notes. The following peculiarities in the autograph have not been adhered to in the present edition:

(1) As staccato-marks we find in part dashes, in part dots. But it does not appear to have been the composer's intention to indicate different degrees of abbreviation.

(2) The short appoggiaturas, counting among them those which, in the livelier movements, admit of an execution as sixteenth-notes, are written as small sixteenth-notes, or (more rarely) as thirty-second notes. There is no apparent reason for making a distinction between the two. The relatively long appoggiaturas in the *Andante* are given in our text, in conformity with the autograph, as eighth-notes.

(3) In the *Tutti* the direction "col Basso" is almost invariably given in the cembalo-part. As this direction has become meaningless in our day, there had to be made, at the closes of some of the *Soli*, certain slight alterations, giving to both right hand and left a quarter-note for the last chord; whereas Mozart had written an eighth-note for the connection with the orchestral bass. It should be observed that early editions do not always notice the places where the direction "col Basso" is intentionally omitted.

Below are quoted a series of earlier readings, which later made way for the versions contained in our text:

II. Andante

[Measures 12] et seq. In the *Andante* the accompanying parts were frequently refined by later corrections. From the 12th measure onward the bass originally read:

All *heavily* engraved slurs, dots and expression-marks are found in the autograph. The editor's additions are distinguishable by lighter (or smaller) engraving.

To Messrs. Conductor-in-Chief Taubert, Royal Librarian Dr. Kopfermann, and Dr. Erich Prieger, special thanks are due for so kindly furnishing material for the revision of the text.

—Dr. Hans Bischoff
Berlin, 1886.

---

†*[This MMO edition utilizes the 1886 Bischoff edition as its source.]*
*Wherever André is quoted, without special qualification, the score-edition is meant.
‡*[Bischoff originally referred to pages from another edition; we have substituted the proper measure numbers in italics and brackets for easy reference.]*

PIANO CONCERTO IN C MAJOR

FEATURED IN THE MOTION PICTURE 'ELVIRA MADIGAN'

II.

WOLFGANG AMADEUS MOZART
KV467

(1) The direction "pizzicato" is omitted in the Br. & H. score-edition.
(2) In Richault, and the old Br. & H. edition of the parts, we find *e g* instead of *g bb*. See the remark, in the Preface, on the earlier reading of this passage.

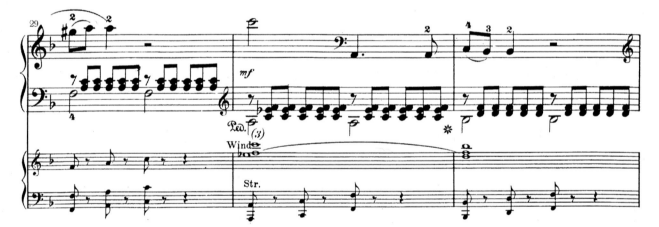

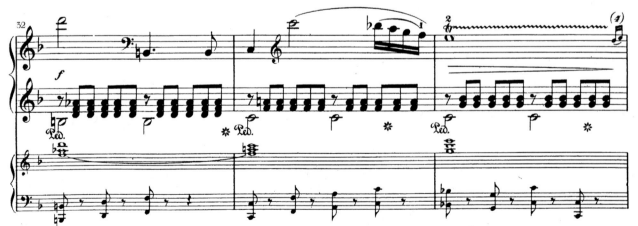

(3) In consequence of a misinterpreted abbreviation in the autograph, several editions (*e. g.*, Richault, Peters, and the old Br. & H. issue) read, instead of the two half-notes, one whole note, *a*. Similar mistakes occur frequently in other places.
(4) Richault, André, and others, omit the afterbeat.

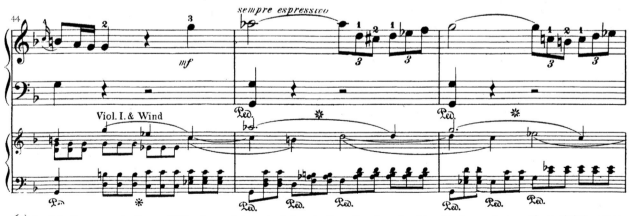

(5) In this figure, and others of like form, it is not plain whether the slur should extend over two or three eighth-notes
(6) The chromatic signs with which the turns are provided, were added by the editor.
(7) These small signs, and the small notes in parenthesis, are given in Richault and the old Br. & H. edition of the
parts. They are lacking in the autograph.

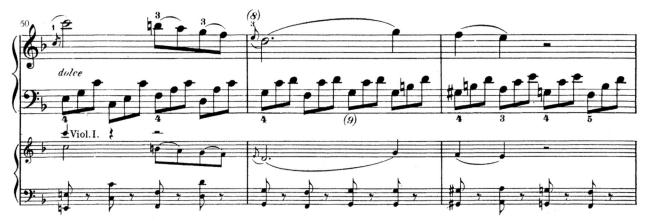

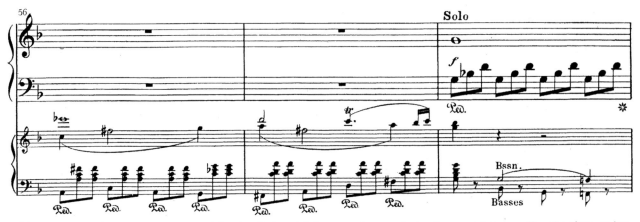

(8) The Br. & H. score does not sufficiently distinguish between long and short appoggiaturas. For the time-value of this *e♯* the editor proposes that of a simple eighth-note.
(9) In this and all similar passages the autograph originally gave, not the Fourth, but the Third. See Preface.

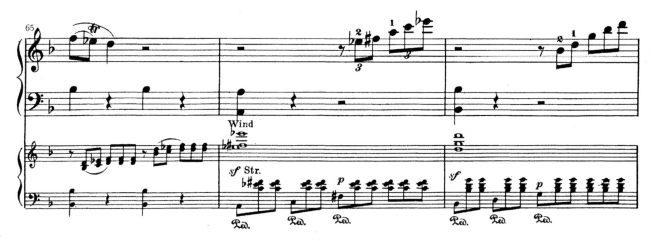

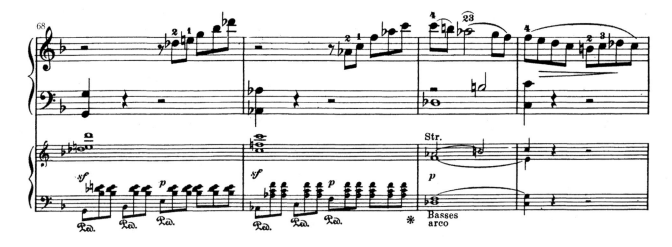

(10) See Note 3.
(11) According to the old Br. & H. edition of the parts, and Richault, the chord also contains the note *d*. This reading is also found in recent issues. The autograph is indistinct.

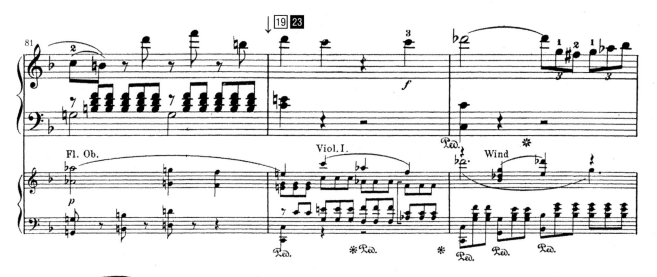

(12) In the editions just mentioned, the note *B* is lacking.

(13) See Note 3.

BRIEF ENCOUNTER
(1945)

SERGEI RACHMANINOV
PIANO CONCERTO NO. 2 IN C MINOR, op. 18

NOTES ON *BRIEF ENCOUNTER*

In his classic 1945 film *Brief Encounter*, director David Lean used Sergei Rachmaninov's Second Piano Concerto throughout the film's soundtrack, leaving an intense impression that lingers strongly to this day. Played in the motion picture by Eileen Joyce, with the Royal Philharmonic Orchestra, the concerto became a sensation once again around the globe at the end of the Second World War. The film recounts, through the eyes of a middle-aged married woman', Laura Jesson (portrayed by Celia Johnson), a startling and unexpected love affair with a doctor, Alec Harvey (Trevor Howard) against the backdrop of war-torn Britain.

Since the film is narrated by Laura Jesson and viewed from her perspective, the Rachmaninov concerto has a particular association with her character and her experience in the story. The flash-back nature of the film enhances the idea of someone recounting a dream, and the music echoes the effect perfectly. Lean repeats sections of the concerto throughout the film, and the overall effect is immersive for the audience.

Because this concerto uncannily nurtures a combination of nostalgia, missed opportunity, joy and doom, it is particularly evocative of the film's narrative and emotional themes. Particularly within the context of the Second World War, when people felt they had little control over their fates, and indeed became suddenly willing to take what would previously have been unthinkable leaps into the world of chance, both the film and its score retain an extreme relevance to their time. Despite the vastly different mores of present-day Western society, the film remains tremendously powerful and affecting. Viewing the film one or more times before playing alongside this album may bring added interpretational perspective for any pianist.

Cues are shown in the accompanying score in circle notation, with each cue's description, start and stop points indicated. For the sake of compactness, and since many sections are repeated and scattered throughout the film, we have structured the compact disc in solid blocks of music, with the various cues given track-breaks for your listening and playing convenience. Though in terms of the original composition this makes the most sense, below is an alternative table showing the film's music cues in their order of appearance in the film, so that you can study, listen to and play this album's selections in this format as well.

—*Michael Norell*

CUE/DESCRIPTION	PAGE	COMPLETE TRACK	MINUS TRACK
Cue 1: Main Title (measure 1)	17	1	22
Cue 2: Drifting, on train/Chatterbox Dolly (m297)	37	9	
Cue 2b: continuation (repeat of Cue 2) (m297)	37	9	
Cue 3: This can't last (closing eyes on the train) (m148)	55	15	35
Cue 4: At the flat with Fred/crosswords/radio (m271 (N.11))	34	7	28
Cue 5: The Flashback: an act of kindness (m133)	27	4	25
Cue 6: Like a Little Boy (m122)	63	18	38
Cue 7: I've enjoyed my afternoon enormously (m310)	67	19	39
Cue 8: Drifting on the train/An accident (m326)	67	20	40
Cue 9: Segue: to the train (m368)	71	21	41
Cue 10: Boating at the Botanical Garden after the pictures (m93)	23	3	24
Cue 11: Kiss at the platform/Dream (m243)	32	6	27
Cue 12: On the train (m42)	58	16	36
Cue 13d: Fantasy holiday (latter portion) (m315)	37	10	30
Cue 14: Mary Norton/The lie/At mirror (m159)	30	5	26
Cue 15: Alibi complete/next meeting (m293)	36	8	29
Cue 16: Winter love/second thoughts (m106)	63	17	37
Cue 17: Ditching the train/return to Alec (m27)	19	2	23
Cue 18: Escape through the night/phone home to Fred (m105)	48	12	32
Cue 19: Wandering/Cigarette at War Memorial/Back to the Station (m128)	53	13	33
Cue 20: On platform with Alec/Africa/Montage to Thursday (p/u to m16)	41	11	31
Cue 21: Last goodbye/full circle/Dolly (m133)	53	14	34
Cue 22: No courage/back to the refreshment bar/Fred (m310)	67	19	39

Highlights from

PIANO CONCERTO № 2

as used in the Motion Picture
Brief Encounter

SECTION I

↓① Main Title

↓ 1 22

Sergei Rachmaninov (1873-1943)
op.18

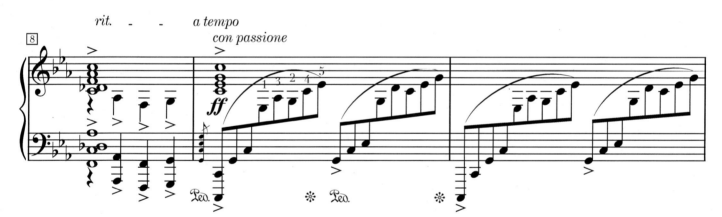

*) When Rachmaninov recorded the Second Concerto with Leopold Stokowski in 1929,
he deviated from his score here: the bottom note of each bass chord in measures 2-8 is sounded first,
treated as a subtle grace note before the beat.

MMO 3093

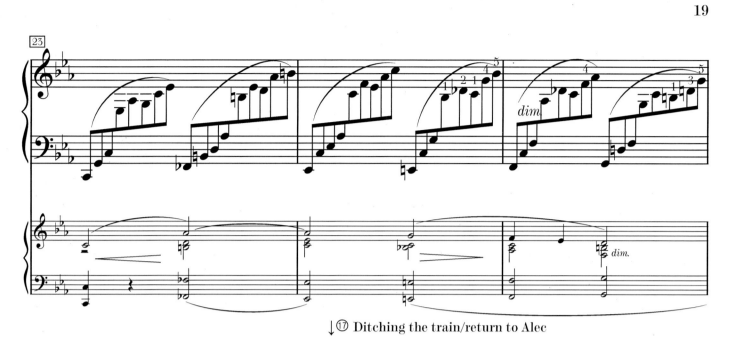

↓⑰ **Ditching the train/return to Alec**

↓ 2 23

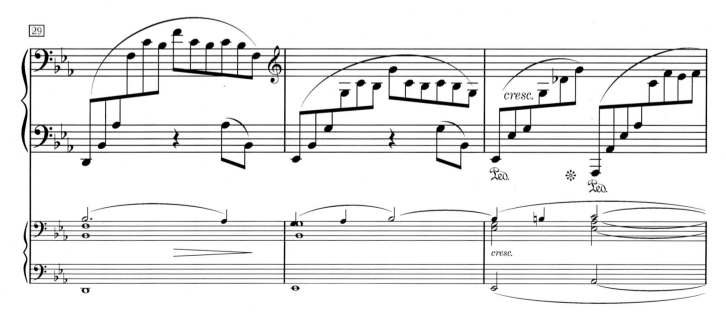

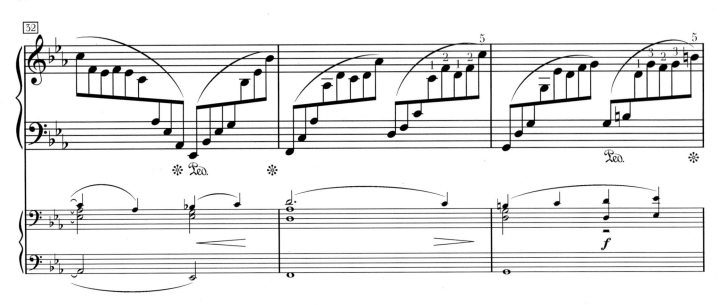

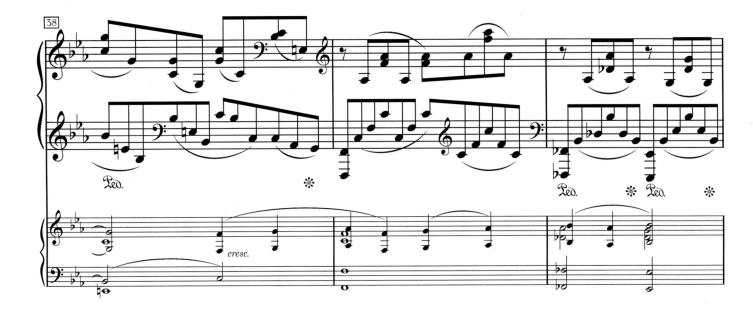

↓End Cue ①

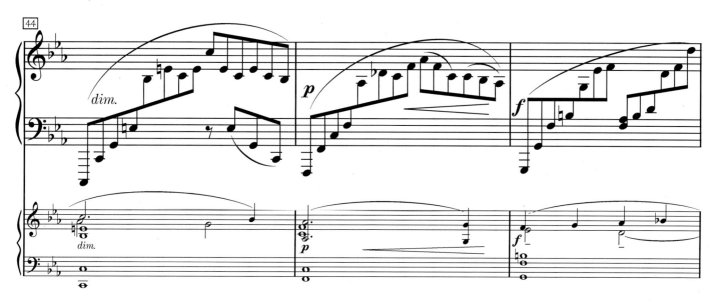

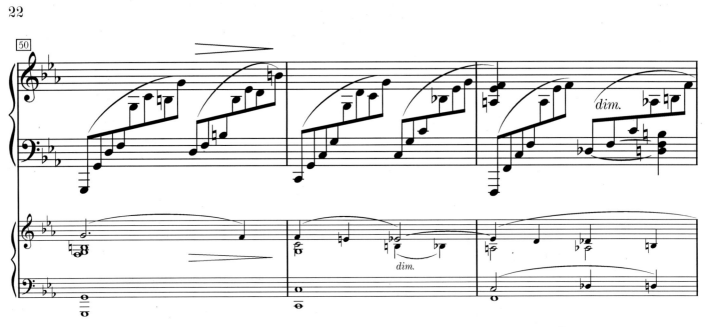

↓End Cue ⑰

3 espressivo

etc...

SECTION II

↓ ⑩ Boating at the Botanical Gardens

↓ 3 24

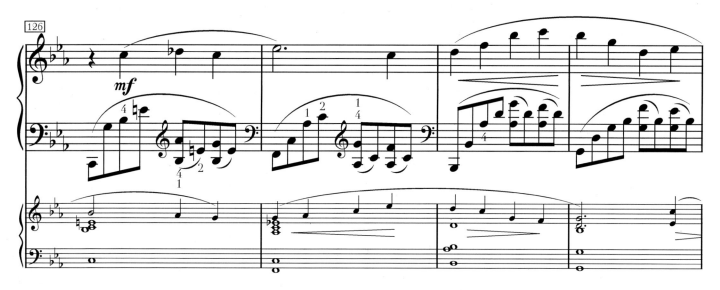

↓⑤ **Flashback: an act of kindness**

↓4 25

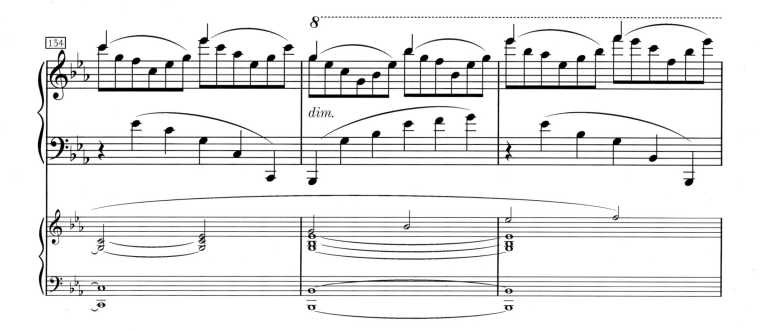

Un poco più mosso ($\mathord{\text{♩}} = 72$)

↓End Cue ⑩

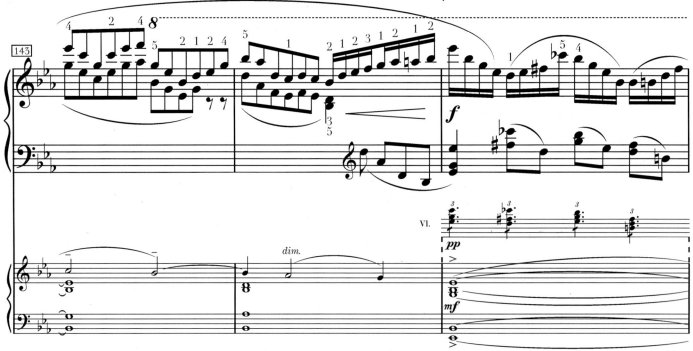

↓End Cue ⑩

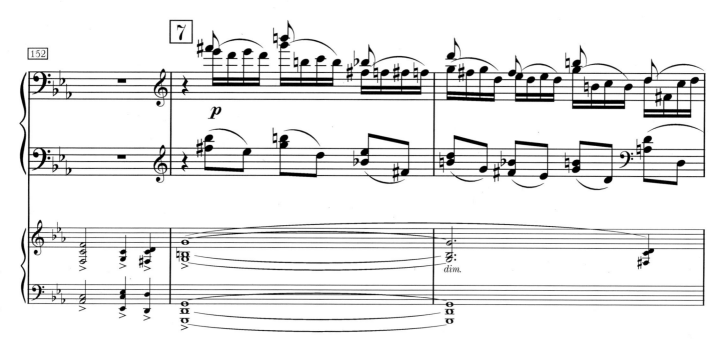

↓⑭ Mary Norton/the lie/mirror

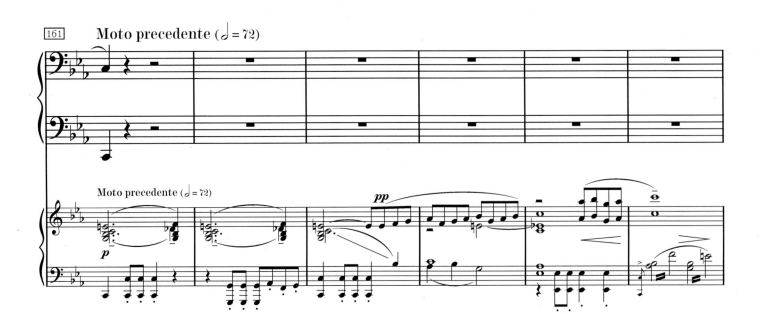

↓End Cue ⑭
Più vivo (♩ = 76)

etc...

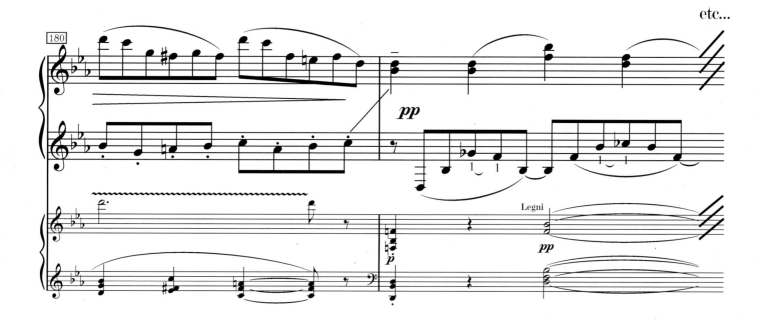

↓⑪ Kiss at the platform/Dream

Maestoso (alla marcia)

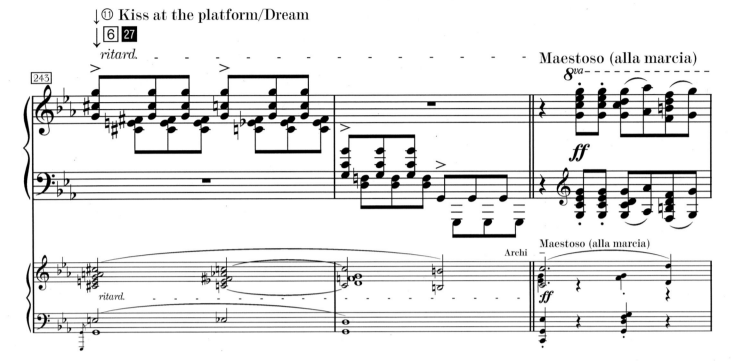

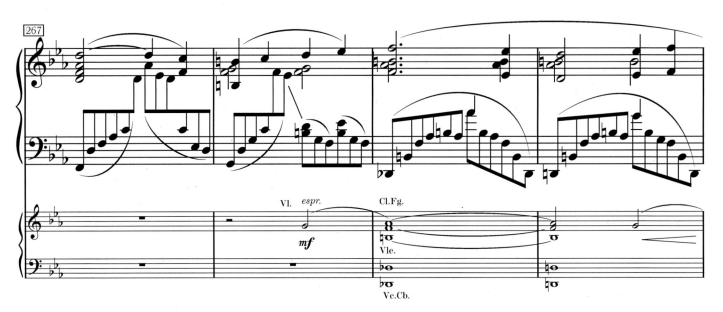

↓④ **At the flat with Fred/crosswords/radio**

↓ 7 28

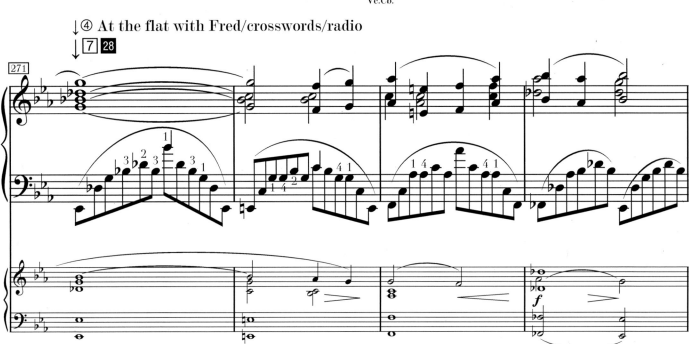

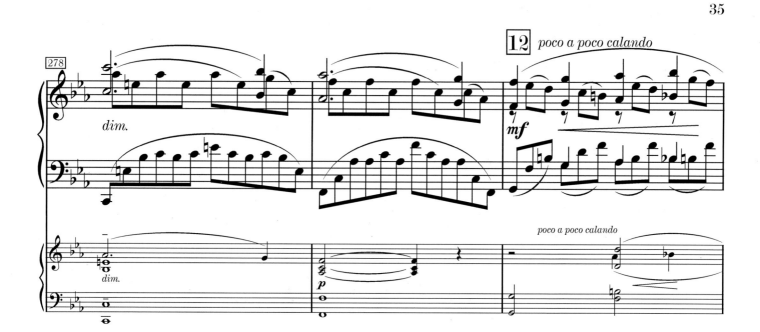

↓⑮ **Alibi complete/next meeting**

↓ 8 29

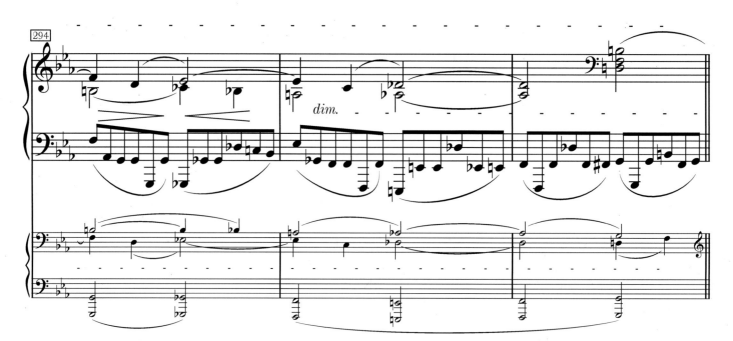

↓End Cue ⑮
↓② Drifting, on train/Chatterbox Dolly
↓9

13
297

Moderato (♩=69)

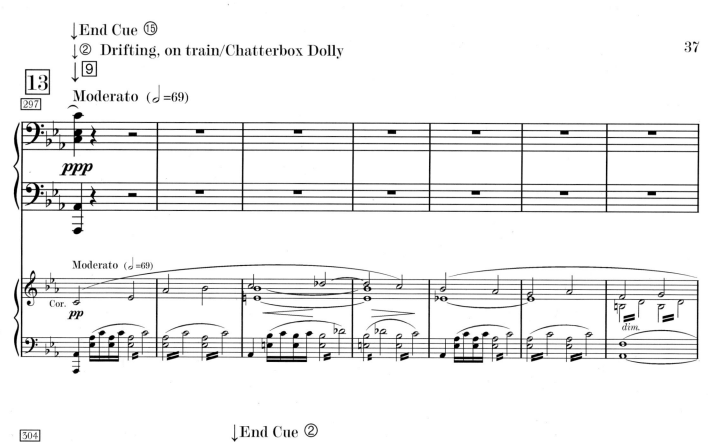

304

↓End Cue ②

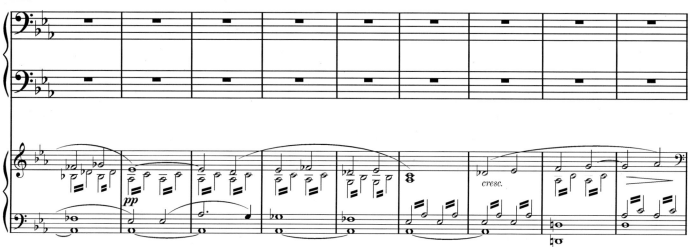

↓⑬d Fantasy holiday (latter portion)
↓10 **30**

313

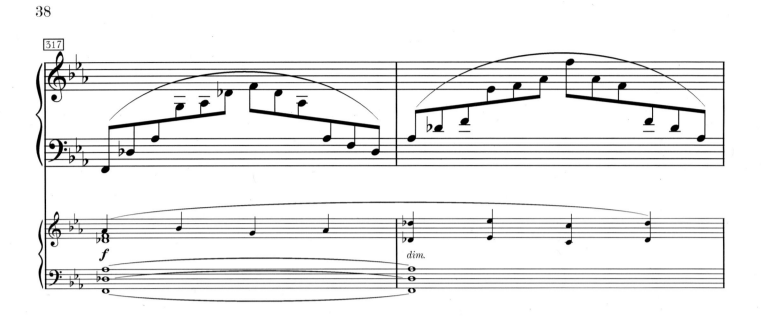

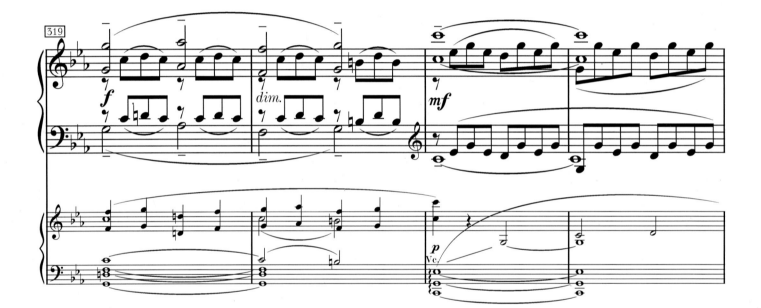

↓End Cue ⑬d

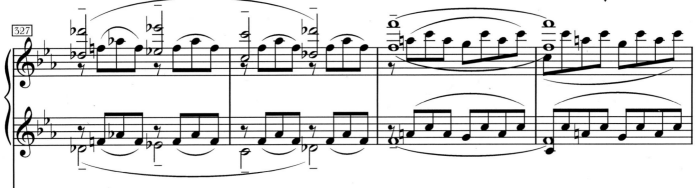

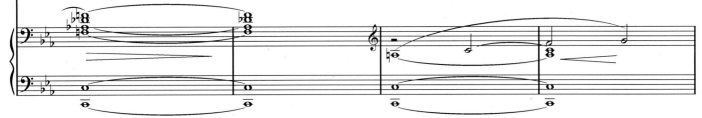

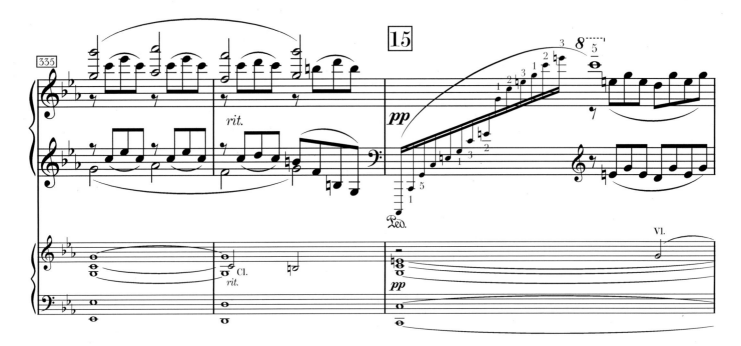

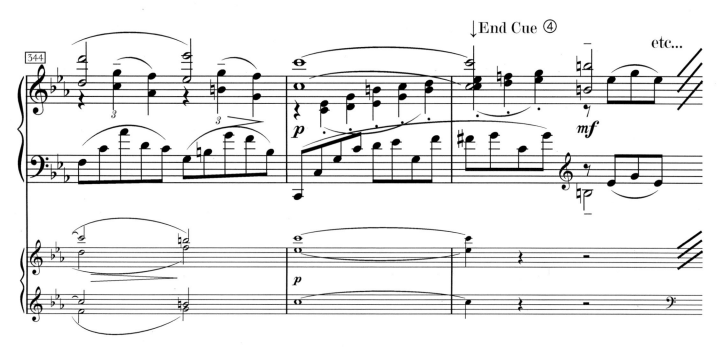

SECTION IV

↓⑳ On the platform with Alec/Arica/Montage to Thusday

18

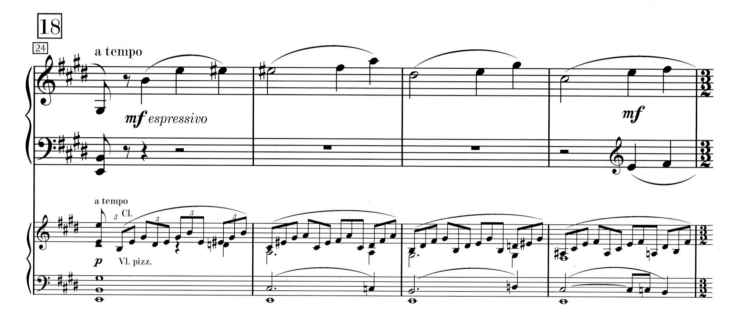

Un poco più animato

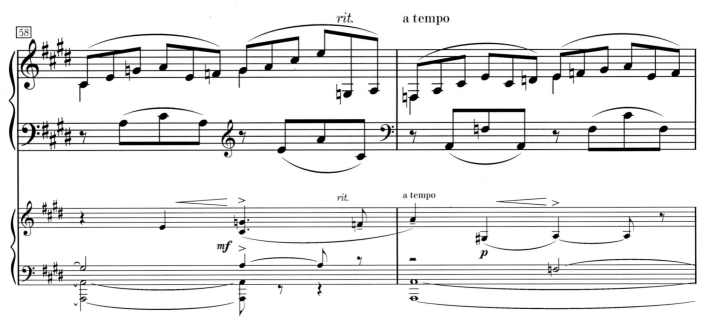

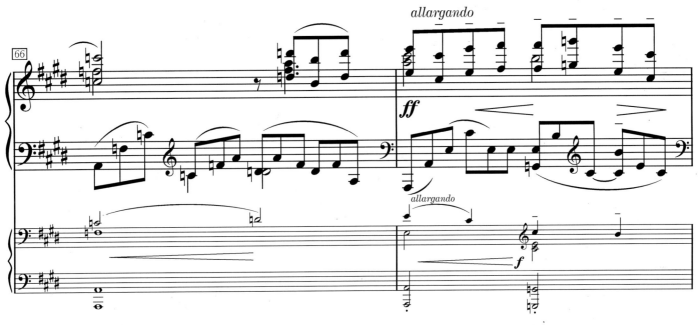

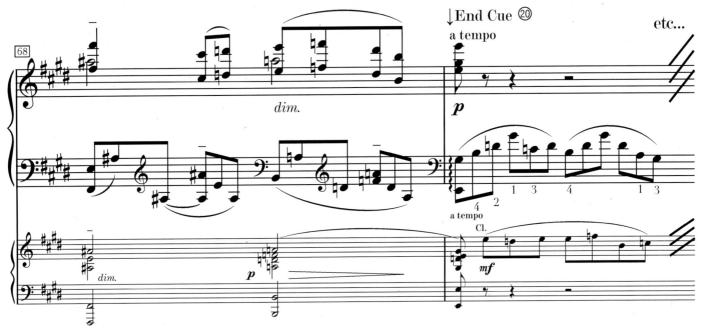

SECTION V

↓⑱ Escape through the night/phone home to Fred

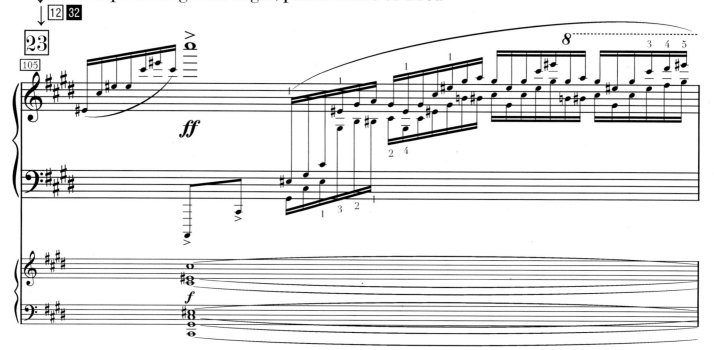

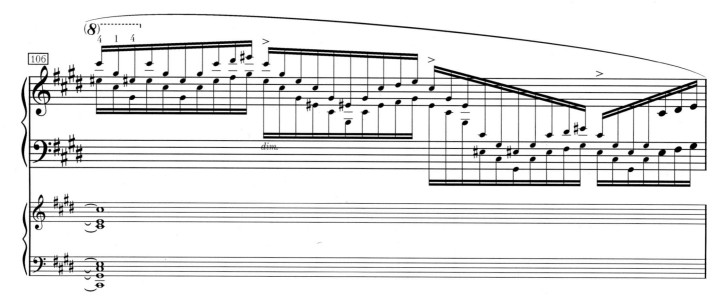

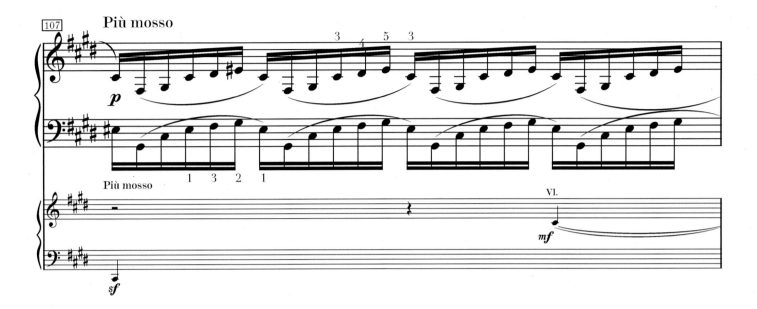

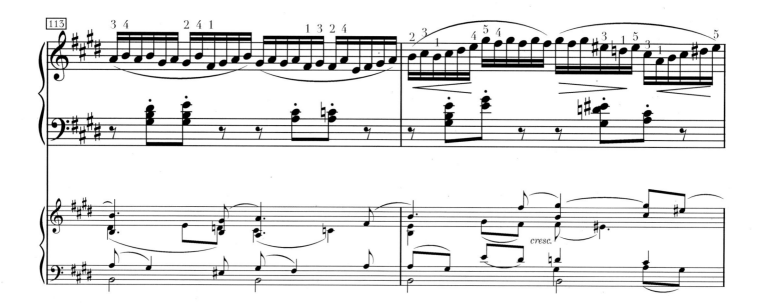

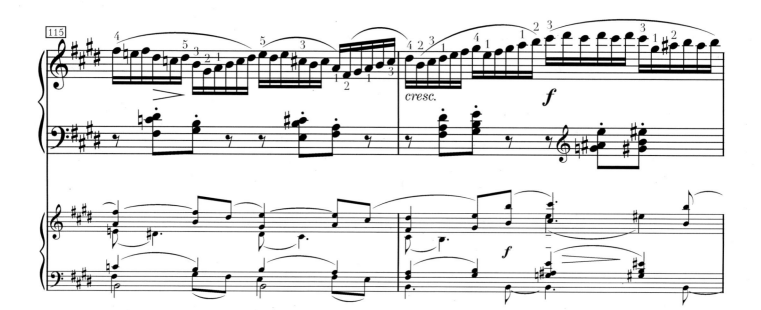

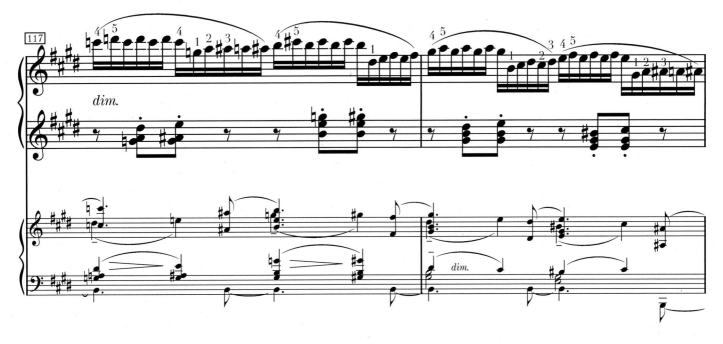

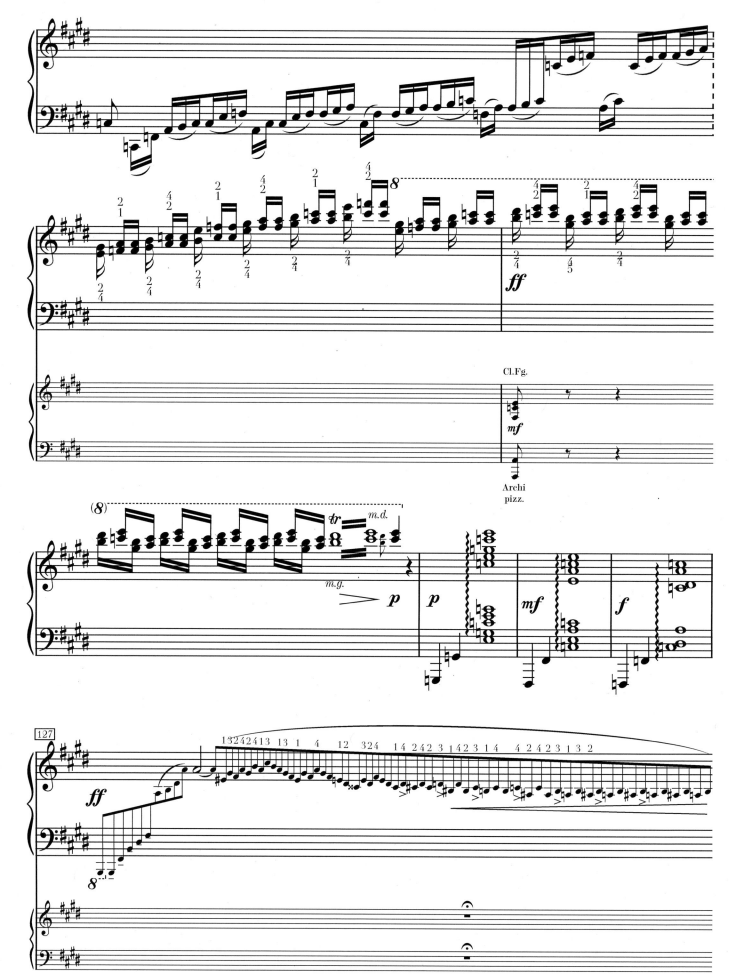

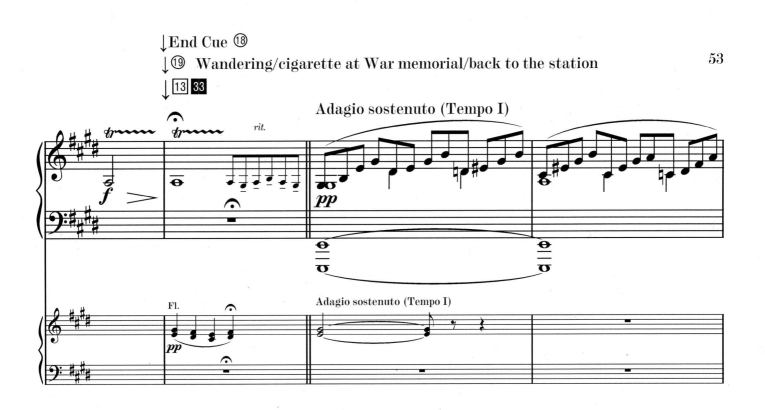

↓End Cue ⑱

↓⑲ Wandering/cigarette at War memorial/back to the station

↓ 13 33

Adagio sostenuto (Tempo I)

Adagio sostenuto (Tempo I)

Fl.

↓㉑ Last goodbye/full circle/Dolly

↓ 14 34

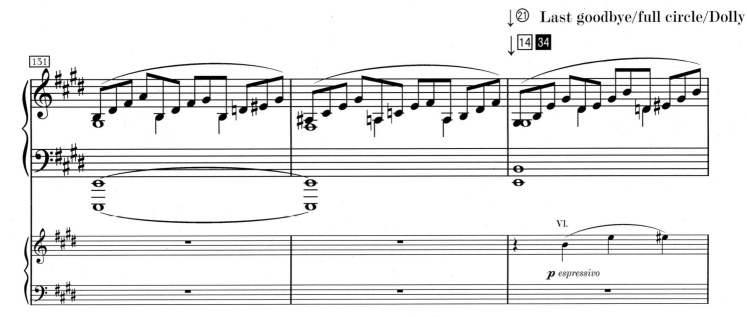

Vl.

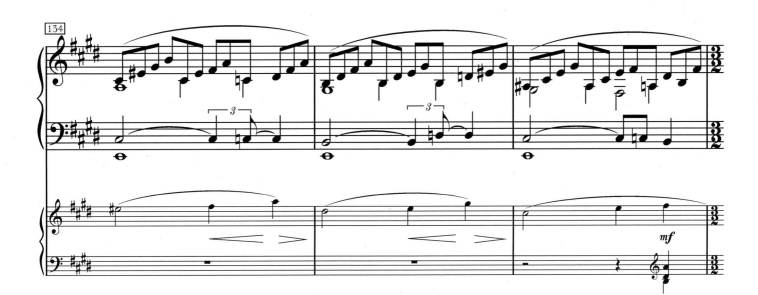

26

↓End Cue ⑲
↓③ This can't last

↓End Cue ③

End Cue ㉑↓

(mvmt III.)
(Allegro scherzando)

SECTION VI

↓ ⑫ On the train

↓ 16 36

28

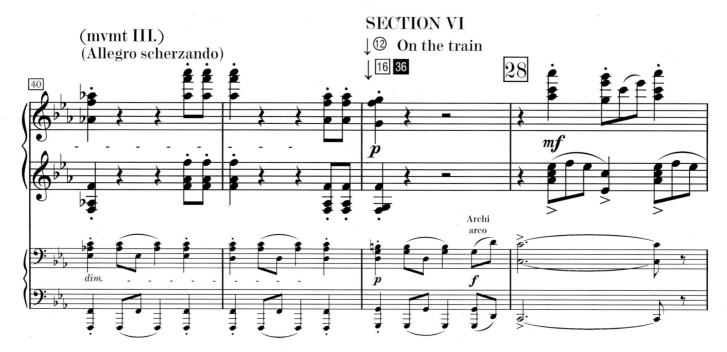

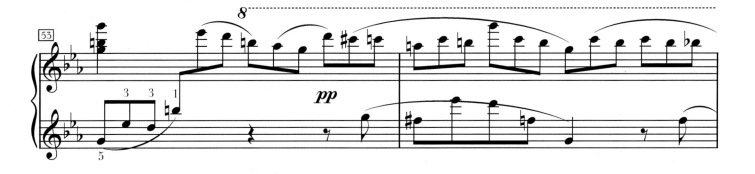

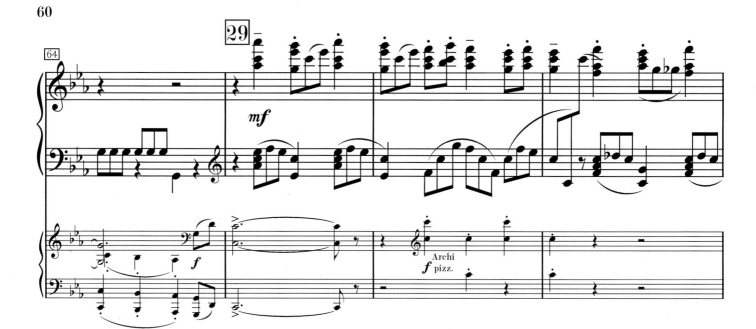

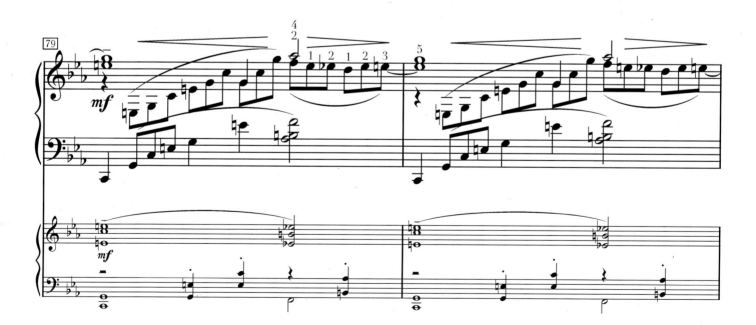

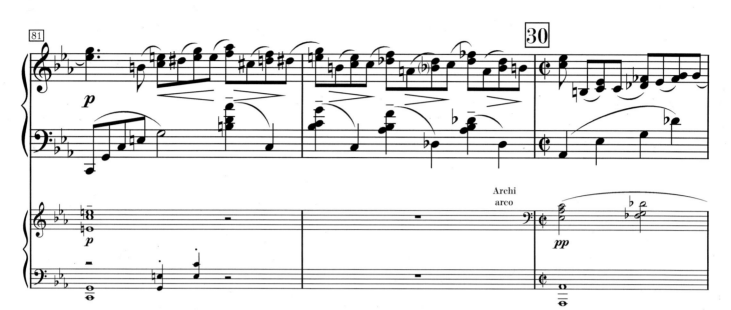

SECTION VII

↓⑯ Winter love/second thoughts

↓ 17 37

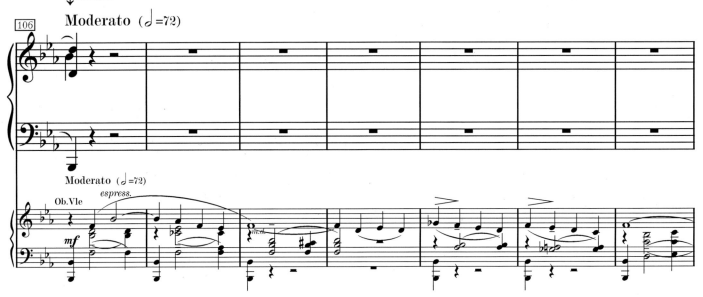

↓⑥ Like a little boy

31 ↓ 18 38

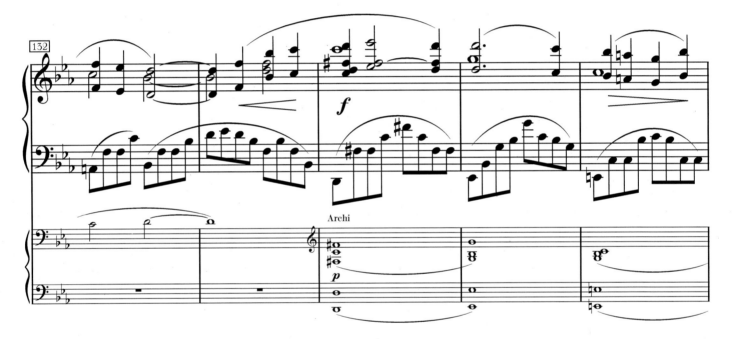

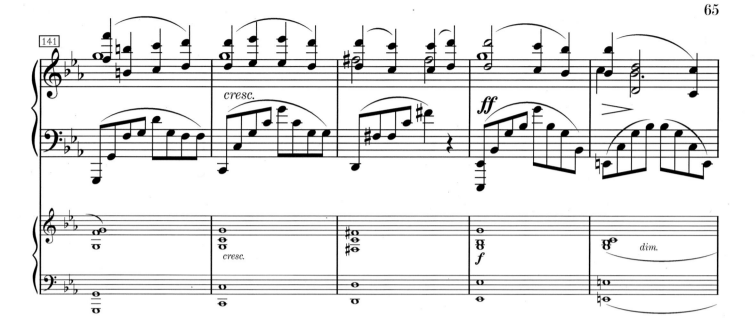

↓End Cue ⑥

32 Meno mosso (♩ = 48)

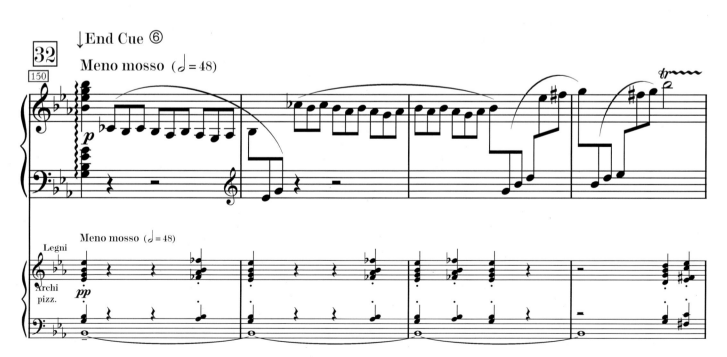

↓End Cue ⑯

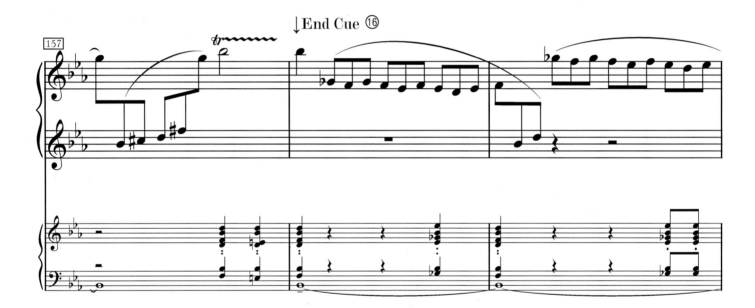

etc...

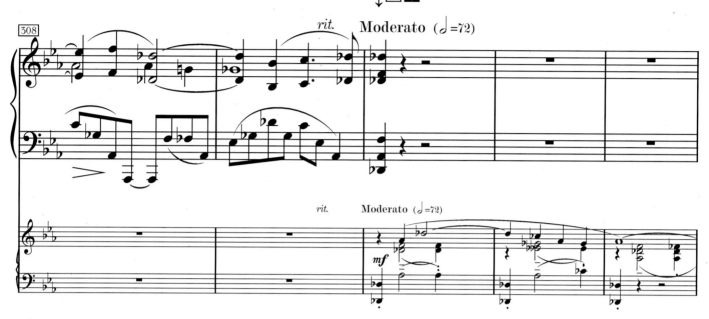

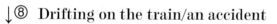

↓ ⑧ Drifting on the train/an accident

↓ 20 40

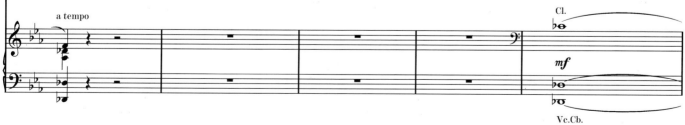

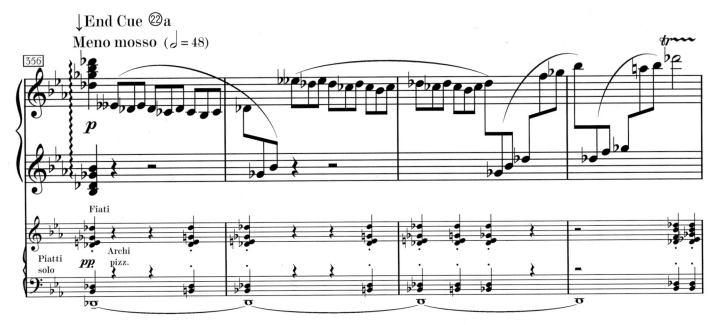

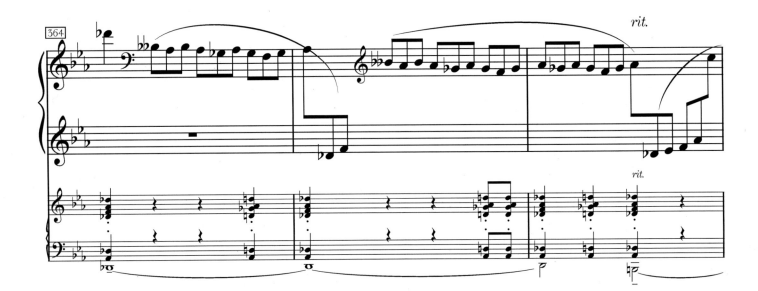

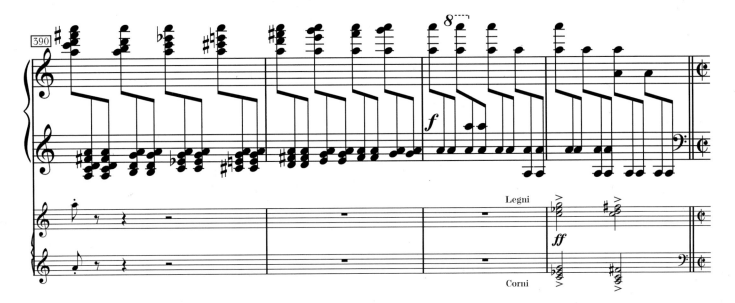

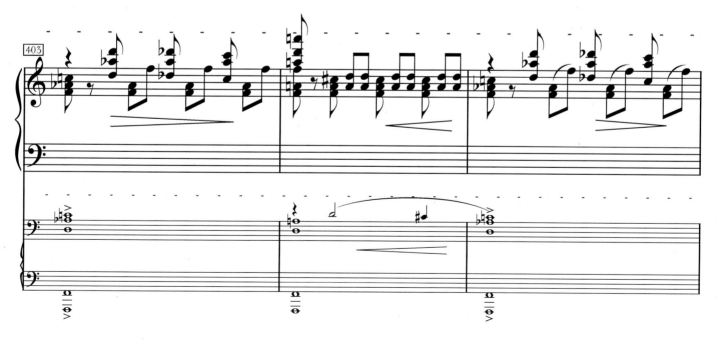

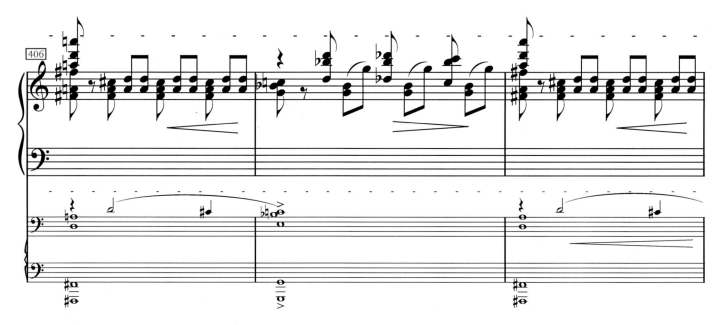

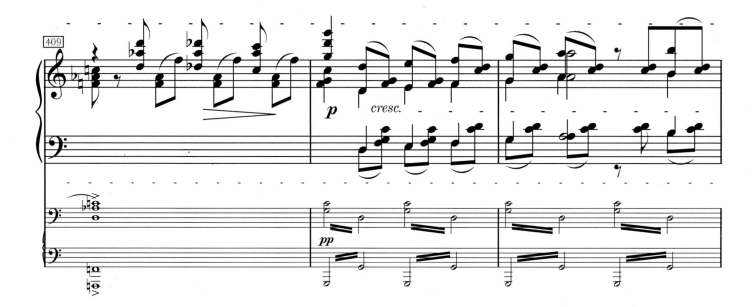

End Cue ⑨↓ etc...

MUSIC MINUS ONE
50 Executive Boulevard
Elmsford, New York 10523-1325
800-669-7464 (U.S.)/914-592-1188 (International)

www.musicminusone.com
e-mail: info@musicminusone.com

MMO 3093   Pub. No. 940   Printed in Canada